AUTISM PLANNER WORKBOOK

A 52 WEEK WORKBOOK FOR PARENTS
TO KEEP TRACK OF THERAPY GOALS,
APPOINTMENTS, AND ACTIVITIES

DYAN ROBSON - ANDNEXTCOMESL.COM

Autism Planner Workbook

Copyright © 2017 Dyan Robson

All rights reserved.

For more autism resources, please visit: http://www.andnextcomesL.com

HOW TO:
USE THIS AUTISM PLANNER WORKBOOK

This autism planner workbook is intended for parents of children with autism and/or sensory issues. It is a blank planner to keep track of sensory activities, appointments, meetings, social goals, speech goals, and more!

In this workbook you will find:

- Two pages per week dedicated to planning out your child's week

- Sections dedicated to recording what goals you would like to focus on during the week with your child, including social skills, speech and communication skills, and sensory goals

- Section dedicated to planning out some activities to try with your child during the week, organized by sensory categories, and includes spots for social skills and speech/language activities

- Section dedicated to keeping track of all those appointments and meetings coming up during the week

- Sections dedicated to reflecting on the past week where challenges, successes, and milestones can be recorded

By the end of the year, you will have a comprehensive book of documentation on your child's progress that can be shared with therapists, doctors, psychologists, teachers, and other support staff.

WEEK 1:
GOALS & OVERVIEW

SPEECH & COMMUNICATION

SOCIAL SKILLS

SENSORY & O.T.

APPOINTMENTS

MONDAY:

TUESDAY:

WEDNESDAY:

THURSDAY:

FRIDAY:

SATURDAY:

SUNDAY:

FINE MOTOR:

VESTIBULAR/PROPRIOCEPTIVE:

TACTILE:

VISUAL:

ORAL MOTOR:

AUDITORY:

SPEECH & LANGUAGE:

SOCIAL SKILLS:

SENSORY & THERAPY ACTIVITY IDEAS

THIS WEEK'S CHALLENGES

THIS WEEK'S HIGHLIGHTS

OTHER COMMENTS

WEEK 2:
GOALS & OVERVIEW

SPEECH & COMMUNICATION

SOCIAL SKILLS

SENSORY & O.T.

APPOINTMENTS

MONDAY:

TUESDAY:

WEDNESDAY:

THURSDAY:

FRIDAY:

SATURDAY:

SUNDAY:

FINE MOTOR:

VESTIBULAR/PROPRIOCEPTIVE:

TACTILE:

VISUAL:

ORAL MOTOR:

AUDITORY:

SPEECH & LANGUAGE:

SOCIAL SKILLS:

SENSORY & THERAPY ACTIVITY IDEAS

THIS WEEK'S CHALLENGES

THIS WEEK'S HIGHLIGHTS

OTHER COMMENTS

WEEK 3:
GOALS & OVERVIEW

SPEECH & COMMUNICATION

SOCIAL SKILLS

SENSORY & O.T.

APPOINTMENTS

MONDAY:

TUESDAY:

WEDNESDAY:

THURSDAY:

FRIDAY:

SATURDAY:

SUNDAY:

WEEK 3:
IDEAS & REVIEW

FINE MOTOR:

VESTIBULAR/PROPRIOCEPTIVE:

TACTILE:

VISUAL:

ORAL MOTOR:

AUDITORY:

SPEECH & LANGUAGE:

SOCIAL SKILLS:

SENSORY & THERAPY ACTIVITY IDEAS

THIS WEEK'S CHALLENGES

THIS WEEK'S HIGHLIGHTS

OTHER COMMENTS

WEEK 4:
GOALS & OVERVIEW

SPEECH & COMMUNICATION

SOCIAL SKILLS

SENSORY & O.T.

APPOINTMENTS

MONDAY:

TUESDAY:

WEDNESDAY:

THURSDAY:

FRIDAY:

SATURDAY:

SUNDAY:

FINE MOTOR:

VESTIBULAR/PROPRIOCEPTIVE:

TACTILE:

VISUAL:

ORAL MOTOR:

AUDITORY:

SPEECH & LANGUAGE:

SOCIAL SKILLS:

SENSORY & THERAPY ACTIVITY IDEAS

WEEK 4:
IDEAS & REVIEW

THIS WEEK'S CHALLENGES

THIS WEEK'S HIGHLIGHTS

OTHER COMMENTS

WEEK 5:
GOALS & OVERVIEW

SPEECH & COMMUNICATION

SOCIAL SKILLS

SENSORY & O.T.

APPOINTMENTS

MONDAY:

TUESDAY:

WEDNESDAY:

THURSDAY:

FRIDAY:

SATURDAY:

SUNDAY:

FINE MOTOR:

VESTIBULAR/PROPRIOCEPTIVE:

TACTILE:

VISUAL:

ORAL MOTOR:

AUDITORY:

SPEECH & LANGUAGE:

SOCIAL SKILLS:

SENSORY & THERAPY ACTIVITY IDEAS

THIS WEEK'S CHALLENGES

THIS WEEK'S HIGHLIGHTS

OTHER COMMENTS

WEEK 6:
GOALS & OVERVIEW

SPEECH & COMMUNICATION

SOCIAL SKILLS

SENSORY & O.T.

APPOINTMENTS

MONDAY:

TUESDAY:

WEDNESDAY:

THURSDAY:

FRIDAY:

SATURDAY:

SUNDAY:

FINE MOTOR:

VESTIBULAR/PROPRIOCEPTIVE:

TACTILE:

VISUAL:

ORAL MOTOR:

AUDITORY:

SPEECH & LANGUAGE:

SOCIAL SKILLS:

SENSORY & THERAPY ACTIVITY IDEAS

WEEK 6:
IDEAS & REVIEW

THIS WEEK'S CHALLENGES

THIS WEEK'S HIGHLIGHTS

OTHER COMMENTS

15

WEEK 7:
GOALS & OVERVIEW

SPEECH & COMMUNICATION

SOCIAL SKILLS

SENSORY & O.T.

APPOINTMENTS

MONDAY:

TUESDAY:

WEDNESDAY:

THURSDAY:

FRIDAY:

SATURDAY:

SUNDAY:

FINE MOTOR:

VESTIBULAR/PROPRIOCEPTIVE:

TACTILE:

VISUAL:

ORAL MOTOR:

AUDITORY:

SPEECH & LANGUAGE:

SOCIAL SKILLS:

SENSORY & THERAPY ACTIVITY IDEAS

WEEK 7:
IDEAS & REVIEW

THIS WEEK'S CHALLENGES

THIS WEEK'S HIGHLIGHTS

OTHER COMMENTS

WEEK 8:
GOALS & OVERVIEW

SPEECH & COMMUNICATION

SOCIAL SKILLS

SENSORY & O.T.

APPOINTMENTS

MONDAY:

TUESDAY:

WEDNESDAY:

THURSDAY:

FRIDAY:

SATURDAY:

SUNDAY:

FINE MOTOR:

VESTIBULAR/PROPRIOCEPTIVE:

TACTILE:

VISUAL:

ORAL MOTOR:

AUDITORY:

SPEECH & LANGUAGE:

SOCIAL SKILLS:

SENSORY & THERAPY ACTIVITY IDEAS

WEEK 8:
IDEAS & REVIEW

THIS WEEK'S CHALLENGES

THIS WEEK'S HIGHLIGHTS

OTHER COMMENTS

WEEK 9:
GOALS & OVERVIEW

SPEECH & COMMUNICATION

SOCIAL SKILLS

SENSORY & O.T.

APPOINTMENTS

MONDAY:

TUESDAY:

WEDNESDAY:

THURSDAY:

FRIDAY:

SATURDAY:

SUNDAY:

WEEK 9:
IDEAS & REVIEW

FINE MOTOR:

VESTIBULAR/PROPRIOCEPTIVE:

TACTILE:

VISUAL:

ORAL MOTOR:

AUDITORY:

SPEECH & LANGUAGE:

SOCIAL SKILLS:

SENSORY & THERAPY ACTIVITY IDEAS

THIS WEEK'S CHALLENGES

THIS WEEK'S HIGHLIGHTS

OTHER COMMENTS

WEEK 10:
GOALS & OVERVIEW

SPEECH & COMMUNICATION

SOCIAL SKILLS

SENSORY & O.T.

APPOINTMENTS

MONDAY:

TUESDAY:

WEDNESDAY:

THURSDAY:

FRIDAY:

SATURDAY:

SUNDAY:

FINE MOTOR:

VESTIBULAR/PROPRIOCEPTIVE:

TACTILE:

VISUAL:

ORAL MOTOR:

AUDITORY:

SPEECH & LANGUAGE:

SOCIAL SKILLS:

SENSORY & THERAPY ACTIVITY IDEAS

WEEK 10:
IDEAS & REVIEW

THIS WEEK'S CHALLENGES

THIS WEEK'S HIGHLIGHTS

OTHER COMMENTS

WEEK 11:
GOALS & OVERVIEW

SPEECH & COMMUNICATION

SOCIAL SKILLS

SENSORY & O.T.

APPOINTMENTS

MONDAY:

TUESDAY:

WEDNESDAY:

THURSDAY:

FRIDAY:

SATURDAY:

SUNDAY:

FINE MOTOR:

VESTIBULAR/PROPRIOCEPTIVE:

TACTILE:

VISUAL:

ORAL MOTOR:

AUDITORY:

SPEECH & LANGUAGE:

SOCIAL SKILLS:

SENSORY & THERAPY ACTIVITY IDEAS

THIS WEEK'S CHALLENGES

THIS WEEK'S HIGHLIGHTS

OTHER COMMENTS

WEEK 12:
GOALS & OVERVIEW

SPEECH & COMMUNICATION

SOCIAL SKILLS

SENSORY & O.T.

APPOINTMENTS

MONDAY:

TUESDAY:

WEDNESDAY:

THURSDAY:

FRIDAY:

SATURDAY:

SUNDAY:

FINE MOTOR:

VESTIBULAR/PROPRIOCEPTIVE:

TACTILE:

VISUAL:

ORAL MOTOR:

AUDITORY:

SPEECH & LANGUAGE:

SOCIAL SKILLS:

SENSORY & THERAPY ACTIVITY IDEAS

WEEK 12:
IDEAS & REVIEW

THIS WEEK'S CHALLENGES

THIS WEEK'S HIGHLIGHTS

OTHER COMMENTS

WEEK 13:
GOALS & OVERVIEW

SPEECH & COMMUNICATION

SOCIAL SKILLS

SENSORY & O.T.

APPOINTMENTS

MONDAY:

TUESDAY:

WEDNESDAY:

THURSDAY:

FRIDAY:

SATURDAY:

SUNDAY:

FINE MOTOR:

VESTIBULAR/PROPRIOCEPTIVE:

TACTILE:

VISUAL:

ORAL MOTOR:

AUDITORY:

SPEECH & LANGUAGE:

SOCIAL SKILLS:

SENSORY & THERAPY ACTIVITY IDEAS

WEEK 13:
IDEAS & REVIEW

THIS WEEK'S CHALLENGES

THIS WEEK'S HIGHLIGHTS

OTHER COMMENTS

WEEK 14:
GOALS & OVERVIEW

SPEECH & COMMUNICATION

SOCIAL SKILLS

SENSORY & O.T.

APPOINTMENTS

MONDAY:

TUESDAY:

WEDNESDAY:

THURSDAY:

FRIDAY:

SATURDAY:

SUNDAY:

FINE MOTOR:

VESTIBULAR/PROPRIOCEPTIVE:

TACTILE:

VISUAL:

ORAL MOTOR:

AUDITORY:

SPEECH & LANGUAGE:

SOCIAL SKILLS:

SENSORY & THERAPY ACTIVITY IDEAS

THIS WEEK'S CHALLENGES

THIS WEEK'S HIGHLIGHTS

OTHER COMMENTS

WEEK 15:
GOALS & OVERVIEW

SPEECH & COMMUNICATION

SOCIAL SKILLS

SENSORY & O.T.

APPOINTMENTS

MONDAY:

TUESDAY:

WEDNESDAY:

THURSDAY:

FRIDAY:

SATURDAY:

SUNDAY:

FINE MOTOR:

VESTIBULAR/PROPRIOCEPTIVE:

TACTILE:

VISUAL:

ORAL MOTOR:

AUDITORY:

SPEECH & LANGUAGE:

SOCIAL SKILLS:

SENSORY & THERAPY ACTIVITY IDEAS

WEEK 15:
IDEAS & REVIEW

THIS WEEK'S CHALLENGES

THIS WEEK'S HIGHLIGHTS

OTHER COMMENTS

WEEK 16:
GOALS & OVERVIEW

SPEECH & COMMUNICATION

SOCIAL SKILLS

SENSORY & O.T.

APPOINTMENTS

MONDAY:

TUESDAY:

WEDNESDAY:

THURSDAY:

FRIDAY:

SATURDAY:

SUNDAY:

FINE MOTOR:

VESTIBULAR/PROPRIOCEPTIVE:

TACTILE:

VISUAL:

ORAL MOTOR:

AUDITORY:

SPEECH & LANGUAGE:

SOCIAL SKILLS:

SENSORY & THERAPY ACTIVITY IDEAS

THIS WEEK'S CHALLENGES

THIS WEEK'S HIGHLIGHTS

OTHER COMMENTS

WEEK 17:
GOALS & OVERVIEW

SPEECH & COMMUNICATION

SOCIAL SKILLS

SENSORY & O.T.

APPOINTMENTS

MONDAY:

TUESDAY:

WEDNESDAY:

THURSDAY:

FRIDAY:

SATURDAY:

SUNDAY:

FINE MOTOR:

VESTIBULAR/PROPRIOCEPTIVE:

TACTILE:

VISUAL:

ORAL MOTOR:

AUDITORY:

SPEECH & LANGUAGE:

SOCIAL SKILLS:

SENSORY & THERAPY ACTIVITY IDEAS

WEEK 17:
IDEAS & REVIEW

THIS WEEK'S CHALLENGES

THIS WEEK'S HIGHLIGHTS

OTHER COMMENTS

WEEK 18:
GOALS & OVERVIEW

SPEECH & COMMUNICATION

SOCIAL SKILLS

SENSORY & O.T.

APPOINTMENTS

MONDAY:

TUESDAY:

WEDNESDAY:

THURSDAY:

FRIDAY:

SATURDAY:

SUNDAY:

FINE MOTOR:

VESTIBULAR/PROPRIOCEPTIVE:

TACTILE:

VISUAL:

ORAL MOTOR:

AUDITORY:

SPEECH & LANGUAGE:

SOCIAL SKILLS:

SENSORY & THERAPY ACTIVITY IDEAS

WEEK 18:
IDEAS & REVIEW

THIS WEEK'S CHALLENGES

THIS WEEK'S HIGHLIGHTS

OTHER COMMENTS

WEEK 19:
GOALS & OVERVIEW

SPEECH & COMMUNICATION

SOCIAL SKILLS

SENSORY & O.T.

APPOINTMENTS

MONDAY:

TUESDAY:

WEDNESDAY:

THURSDAY:

FRIDAY:

SATURDAY:

SUNDAY:

WEEK 19:
IDEAS & REVIEW

FINE MOTOR:

VESTIBULAR/PROPRIOCEPTIVE:

TACTILE:

VISUAL:

ORAL MOTOR:

AUDITORY:

SPEECH & LANGUAGE:

SOCIAL SKILLS:

SENSORY & THERAPY ACTIVITY IDEAS

THIS WEEK'S CHALLENGES

THIS WEEK'S HIGHLIGHTS

OTHER COMMENTS

WEEK 20:
GOALS & OVERVIEW

SPEECH & COMMUNICATION

SOCIAL SKILLS

SENSORY & O.T.

APPOINTMENTS

MONDAY:

TUESDAY:

WEDNESDAY:

THURSDAY:

FRIDAY:

SATURDAY:

SUNDAY:

FINE MOTOR:

VESTIBULAR/PROPRIOCEPTIVE:

TACTILE:

VISUAL:

ORAL MOTOR:

AUDITORY:

SPEECH & LANGUAGE:

SOCIAL SKILLS:

SENSORY & THERAPY ACTIVITY IDEAS

THIS WEEK'S CHALLENGES

THIS WEEK'S HIGHLIGHTS

OTHER COMMENTS

WEEK 21:
GOALS & OVERVIEW

SPEECH & COMMUNICATION

SOCIAL SKILLS

SENSORY & O.T.

APPOINTMENTS

MONDAY:

TUESDAY:

WEDNESDAY:

THURSDAY:

FRIDAY:

SATURDAY:

SUNDAY:

FINE MOTOR:

VESTIBULAR/PROPRIOCEPTIVE:

TACTILE:

VISUAL:

ORAL MOTOR:

AUDITORY:

SPEECH & LANGUAGE:

SOCIAL SKILLS:

SENSORY & THERAPY ACTIVITY IDEAS

WEEK 21:
IDEAS & REVIEW

THIS WEEK'S CHALLENGES

THIS WEEK'S HIGHLIGHTS

OTHER COMMENTS

WEEK 22:
GOALS & OVERVIEW

SPEECH & COMMUNICATION

SOCIAL SKILLS

SENSORY & O.T.

APPOINTMENTS

MONDAY:

TUESDAY:

WEDNESDAY:

THURSDAY:

FRIDAY:

SATURDAY:

SUNDAY:

FINE MOTOR:

VESTIBULAR/PROPRIOCEPTIVE:

TACTILE:

VISUAL:

ORAL MOTOR:

AUDITORY:

SPEECH & LANGUAGE:

SOCIAL SKILLS:

SENSORY & THERAPY ACTIVITY IDEAS

THIS WEEK'S CHALLENGES

THIS WEEK'S HIGHLIGHTS

OTHER COMMENTS

WEEK 23:
GOALS & OVERVIEW

SPEECH & COMMUNICATION

SOCIAL SKILLS

SENSORY & O.T.

APPOINTMENTS

MONDAY:

TUESDAY:

WEDNESDAY:

THURSDAY:

FRIDAY:

SATURDAY:

SUNDAY:

FINE MOTOR:

VESTIBULAR/PROPRIOCEPTIVE:

TACTILE:

VISUAL:

ORAL MOTOR:

AUDITORY:

SPEECH & LANGUAGE:

SOCIAL SKILLS:

SENSORY & THERAPY ACTIVITY IDEAS

WEEK 23:
IDEAS & REVIEW

THIS WEEK'S CHALLENGES

THIS WEEK'S HIGHLIGHTS

OTHER COMMENTS

WEEK 24:
GOALS & OVERVIEW

SPEECH & COMMUNICATION

SOCIAL SKILLS

SENSORY & O.T.

APPOINTMENTS

MONDAY:

TUESDAY:

WEDNESDAY:

THURSDAY:

FRIDAY:

SATURDAY:

SUNDAY:

WEEK 24:
IDEAS & REVIEW

FINE MOTOR:

VESTIBULAR/PROPRIOCEPTIVE:

TACTILE:

VISUAL:

ORAL MOTOR:

AUDITORY:

SPEECH & LANGUAGE:

SOCIAL SKILLS:

SENSORY & THERAPY ACTIVITY IDEAS

THIS WEEK'S CHALLENGES

THIS WEEK'S HIGHLIGHTS

OTHER COMMENTS

WEEK 25:
GOALS & OVERVIEW

SPEECH & COMMUNICATION

SOCIAL SKILLS

SENSORY & O.T.

APPOINTMENTS

MONDAY:

TUESDAY:

WEDNESDAY:

THURSDAY:

FRIDAY:

SATURDAY:

SUNDAY:

FINE MOTOR:

VESTIBULAR/PROPRIOCEPTIVE:

TACTILE:

VISUAL:

ORAL MOTOR:

AUDITORY:

SPEECH & LANGUAGE:

SOCIAL SKILLS:

SENSORY & THERAPY ACTIVITY IDEAS

WEEK 25:
IDEAS & REVIEW

THIS WEEK'S CHALLENGES

THIS WEEK'S HIGHLIGHTS

OTHER COMMENTS

WEEK 26:
GOALS & OVERVIEW

SPEECH & COMMUNICATION

SOCIAL SKILLS

SENSORY & O.T.

APPOINTMENTS

MONDAY:

TUESDAY:

WEDNESDAY:

THURSDAY:

FRIDAY:

SATURDAY:

SUNDAY:

FINE MOTOR:

VESTIBULAR/PROPRIOCEPTIVE:

TACTILE:

VISUAL:

ORAL MOTOR:

AUDITORY:

SPEECH & LANGUAGE:

SOCIAL SKILLS:

SENSORY & THERAPY ACTIVITY IDEAS

WEEK 26:
IDEAS & REVIEW

THIS WEEK'S CHALLENGES

THIS WEEK'S HIGHLIGHTS

OTHER COMMENTS

WEEK 27:
GOALS & OVERVIEW

SPEECH & COMMUNICATION

SOCIAL SKILLS

SENSORY & O.T.

APPOINTMENTS

MONDAY:

TUESDAY:

WEDNESDAY:

THURSDAY:

FRIDAY:

SATURDAY:

SUNDAY:

FINE MOTOR:

VESTIBULAR/PROPRIOCEPTIVE:

TACTILE:

VISUAL:

ORAL MOTOR:

AUDITORY:

SPEECH & LANGUAGE:

SOCIAL SKILLS:

SENSORY & THERAPY ACTIVITY IDEAS

WEEK 27:
IDEAS & REVIEW

THIS WEEK'S CHALLENGES

THIS WEEK'S HIGHLIGHTS

OTHER COMMENTS

WEEK 28:
GOALS & OVERVIEW

SPEECH & COMMUNICATION

SOCIAL SKILLS

SENSORY & O.T.

APPOINTMENTS

MONDAY:

TUESDAY:

WEDNESDAY:

THURSDAY:

FRIDAY:

SATURDAY:

SUNDAY:

FINE MOTOR:

VESTIBULAR/PROPRIOCEPTIVE:

TACTILE:

VISUAL:

ORAL MOTOR:

AUDITORY:

SPEECH & LANGUAGE:

SOCIAL SKILLS:

SENSORY & THERAPY ACTIVITY IDEAS

THIS WEEK'S CHALLENGES

THIS WEEK'S HIGHLIGHTS

OTHER COMMENTS

WEEK 29:
GOALS & OVERVIEW

SPEECH & COMMUNICATION

SOCIAL SKILLS

SENSORY & O.T.

APPOINTMENTS

MONDAY:

TUESDAY:

WEDNESDAY:

THURSDAY:

FRIDAY:

SATURDAY:

SUNDAY:

FINE MOTOR:

VESTIBULAR/PROPRIOCEPTIVE:

TACTILE:

VISUAL:

ORAL MOTOR:

AUDITORY:

SPEECH & LANGUAGE:

SOCIAL SKILLS:

SENSORY & THERAPY ACTIVITY IDEAS

THIS WEEK'S CHALLENGES

THIS WEEK'S HIGHLIGHTS

OTHER COMMENTS

WEEK 30:
GOALS & OVERVIEW

SPEECH & COMMUNICATION

SOCIAL SKILLS

SENSORY & O.T.

APPOINTMENTS

MONDAY:

TUESDAY:

WEDNESDAY:

THURSDAY:

FRIDAY:

SATURDAY:

SUNDAY:

FINE MOTOR:

VESTIBULAR/PROPRIOCEPTIVE:

TACTILE:

VISUAL:

ORAL MOTOR:

AUDITORY:

SPEECH & LANGUAGE:

SOCIAL SKILLS:

SENSORY & THERAPY ACTIVITY IDEAS

WEEK 30:
IDEAS & REVIEW

THIS WEEK'S CHALLENGES

THIS WEEK'S HIGHLIGHTS

OTHER COMMENTS

WEEK 31:
GOALS & OVERVIEW

SPEECH & COMMUNICATION

SOCIAL SKILLS

SENSORY & O.T.

APPOINTMENTS

MONDAY:

TUESDAY:

WEDNESDAY:

THURSDAY:

FRIDAY:

SATURDAY:

SUNDAY:

FINE MOTOR:

VESTIBULAR/PROPRIOCEPTIVE:

TACTILE:

VISUAL:

ORAL MOTOR:

AUDITORY:

SPEECH & LANGUAGE:

SOCIAL SKILLS:

SENSORY & THERAPY ACTIVITY IDEAS

WEEK 31:
IDEAS & REVIEW

THIS WEEK'S CHALLENGES

THIS WEEK'S HIGHLIGHTS

OTHER COMMENTS

WEEK 32:
GOALS & OVERVIEW

SPEECH & COMMUNICATION

SOCIAL SKILLS

SENSORY & O.T.

APPOINTMENTS

MONDAY:

TUESDAY:

WEDNESDAY:

THURSDAY:

FRIDAY:

SATURDAY:

SUNDAY:

FINE MOTOR:

VESTIBULAR/PROPRIOCEPTIVE:

TACTILE:

VISUAL:

ORAL MOTOR:

AUDITORY:

SPEECH & LANGUAGE:

SOCIAL SKILLS:

SENSORY & THERAPY ACTIVITY IDEAS

WEEK 32:
IDEAS & REVIEW

THIS WEEK'S CHALLENGES

THIS WEEK'S HIGHLIGHTS

OTHER COMMENTS

WEEK 33:
GOALS & OVERVIEW

SPEECH & COMMUNICATION

SOCIAL SKILLS

SENSORY & O.T.

APPOINTMENTS

MONDAY:

TUESDAY:

WEDNESDAY:

THURSDAY:

FRIDAY:

SATURDAY:

SUNDAY:

FINE MOTOR:

VESTIBULAR/PROPRIOCEPTIVE:

TACTILE:

VISUAL:

ORAL MOTOR:

AUDITORY:

SPEECH & LANGUAGE:

SOCIAL SKILLS:

SENSORY & THERAPY ACTIVITY IDEAS

IDEAS & REVIEW

THIS WEEK'S CHALLENGES

THIS WEEK'S HIGHLIGHTS

OTHER COMMENTS

69

WEEK 34:
GOALS & OVERVIEW

SPEECH & COMMUNICATION

SOCIAL SKILLS

SENSORY & O.T.

APPOINTMENTS

MONDAY:

TUESDAY:

WEDNESDAY:

THURSDAY:

FRIDAY:

SATURDAY:

SUNDAY:

FINE MOTOR:

VESTIBULAR/PROPRIOCEPTIVE:

TACTILE:

VISUAL:

ORAL MOTOR:

AUDITORY:

SPEECH & LANGUAGE:

SOCIAL SKILLS:

SENSORY & THERAPY ACTIVITY IDEAS

WEEK 34:
IDEAS & REVIEW

THIS WEEK'S CHALLENGES

THIS WEEK'S HIGHLIGHTS

OTHER COMMENTS

WEEK 35:
GOALS & OVERVIEW

SPEECH & COMMUNICATION

SOCIAL SKILLS

SENSORY & O.T.

APPOINTMENTS

MONDAY:

TUESDAY:

WEDNESDAY:

THURSDAY:

FRIDAY:

SATURDAY:

SUNDAY:

FINE MOTOR:

VESTIBULAR/PROPRIOCEPTIVE:

TACTILE:

VISUAL:

ORAL MOTOR:

AUDITORY:

SPEECH & LANGUAGE:

SOCIAL SKILLS:

SENSORY & THERAPY ACTIVITY IDEAS

WEEK 35:
IDEAS & REVIEW

THIS WEEK'S CHALLENGES

THIS WEEK'S HIGHLIGHTS

OTHER COMMENTS

WEEK 36:
GOALS & OVERVIEW

SPEECH & COMMUNICATION

SOCIAL SKILLS

SENSORY & O.T.

APPOINTMENTS

MONDAY:

TUESDAY:

WEDNESDAY:

THURSDAY:

FRIDAY:

SATURDAY:

SUNDAY:

FINE MOTOR:

VESTIBULAR/PROPRIOCEPTIVE:

TACTILE:

VISUAL:

ORAL MOTOR:

AUDITORY:

SPEECH & LANGUAGE:

SOCIAL SKILLS:

SENSORY & THERAPY ACTIVITY IDEAS

WEEK 36:
IDEAS & REVIEW

THIS WEEK'S CHALLENGES

THIS WEEK'S HIGHLIGHTS

OTHER COMMENTS

WEEK 37:
GOALS & OVERVIEW

SPEECH & COMMUNICATION

SOCIAL SKILLS

SENSORY & O.T.

APPOINTMENTS

MONDAY:

TUESDAY:

WEDNESDAY:

THURSDAY:

FRIDAY:

SATURDAY:

SUNDAY:

FINE MOTOR:

VESTIBULAR/PROPRIOCEPTIVE:

TACTILE:

VISUAL:

ORAL MOTOR:

AUDITORY:

SPEECH & LANGUAGE:

SOCIAL SKILLS:

SENSORY & THERAPY ACTIVITY IDEAS

WEEK 37:
IDEAS & REVIEW

THIS WEEK'S CHALLENGES

THIS WEEK'S HIGHLIGHTS

OTHER COMMENTS

WEEK 38:
GOALS & OVERVIEW

SPEECH & COMMUNICATION

SOCIAL SKILLS

SENSORY & O.T.

APPOINTMENTS

MONDAY:

TUESDAY:

WEDNESDAY:

THURSDAY:

FRIDAY:

SATURDAY:

SUNDAY:

FINE MOTOR:

VESTIBULAR/PROPRIOCEPTIVE:

TACTILE:

VISUAL:

ORAL MOTOR:

AUDITORY:

SPEECH & LANGUAGE:

SOCIAL SKILLS:

SENSORY & THERAPY ACTIVITY IDEAS

WEEK 38:
IDEAS & REVIEW

THIS WEEK'S CHALLENGES

THIS WEEK'S HIGHLIGHTS

OTHER COMMENTS

WEEK 39:
GOALS & OVERVIEW

SPEECH & COMMUNICATION

SOCIAL SKILLS

SENSORY & O.T.

APPOINTMENTS

MONDAY:

TUESDAY:

WEDNESDAY:

THURSDAY:

FRIDAY:

SATURDAY:

SUNDAY:

FINE MOTOR:

VESTIBULAR/PROPRIOCEPTIVE:

TACTILE:

VISUAL:

ORAL MOTOR:

AUDITORY:

SPEECH & LANGUAGE:

SOCIAL SKILLS:

SENSORY & THERAPY ACTIVITY IDEAS

WEEK 39:
IDEAS & REVIEW

THIS WEEK'S CHALLENGES

THIS WEEK'S HIGHLIGHTS

OTHER COMMENTS

WEEK 40:
GOALS & OVERVIEW

SPEECH & COMMUNICATION

SOCIAL SKILLS

SENSORY & O.T.

APPOINTMENTS

MONDAY:

TUESDAY:

WEDNESDAY:

THURSDAY:

FRIDAY:

SATURDAY:

SUNDAY:

FINE MOTOR:

VESTIBULAR/PROPRIOCEPTIVE:

TACTILE:

VISUAL:

ORAL MOTOR:

AUDITORY:

SPEECH & LANGUAGE:

SOCIAL SKILLS:

SENSORY & THERAPY ACTIVITY IDEAS

THIS WEEK'S CHALLENGES

THIS WEEK'S HIGHLIGHTS

OTHER COMMENTS

WEEK 41:
GOALS & OVERVIEW

SPEECH & COMMUNICATION

SOCIAL SKILLS

SENSORY & O.T.

APPOINTMENTS

MONDAY:

TUESDAY:

WEDNESDAY:

THURSDAY:

FRIDAY:

SATURDAY:

SUNDAY:

FINE MOTOR:

VESTIBULAR/PROPRIOCEPTIVE:

TACTILE:

VISUAL:

ORAL MOTOR:

AUDITORY:

SPEECH & LANGUAGE:

SOCIAL SKILLS:

SENSORY & THERAPY ACTIVITY IDEAS

WEEK 41:
IDEAS & REVIEW

THIS WEEK'S CHALLENGES

THIS WEEK'S HIGHLIGHTS

OTHER COMMENTS

WEEK 42:
GOALS & OVERVIEW

SPEECH & COMMUNICATION

SOCIAL SKILLS

SENSORY & O.T.

APPOINTMENTS

MONDAY:

TUESDAY:

WEDNESDAY:

THURSDAY:

FRIDAY:

SATURDAY:

SUNDAY:

FINE MOTOR:

VESTIBULAR/PROPRIOCEPTIVE:

TACTILE:

VISUAL:

ORAL MOTOR:

AUDITORY:

SPEECH & LANGUAGE:

SOCIAL SKILLS:

SENSORY & THERAPY ACTIVITY IDEAS

THIS WEEK'S CHALLENGES

THIS WEEK'S HIGHLIGHTS

OTHER COMMENTS

WEEK 43:
GOALS & OVERVIEW

SPEECH & COMMUNICATION

SOCIAL SKILLS

SENSORY & O.T.

APPOINTMENTS

MONDAY:

TUESDAY:

WEDNESDAY:

THURSDAY:

FRIDAY:

SATURDAY:

SUNDAY:

FINE MOTOR:

VESTIBULAR/PROPRIOCEPTIVE:

TACTILE:

VISUAL:

ORAL MOTOR:

AUDITORY:

SPEECH & LANGUAGE:

SOCIAL SKILLS:

SENSORY & THERAPY ACTIVITY IDEAS

WEEK 43:
IDEAS & REVIEW

THIS WEEK'S CHALLENGES

THIS WEEK'S HIGHLIGHTS

OTHER COMMENTS

WEEK 44:
GOALS & OVERVIEW

SPEECH & COMMUNICATION

SOCIAL SKILLS

SENSORY & O.T.

APPOINTMENTS

MONDAY:

TUESDAY:

WEDNESDAY:

THURSDAY:

FRIDAY:

SATURDAY:

SUNDAY:

FINE MOTOR:

VESTIBULAR/PROPRIOCEPTIVE:

TACTILE:

VISUAL:

ORAL MOTOR:

AUDITORY:

SPEECH & LANGUAGE:

SOCIAL SKILLS:

SENSORY & THERAPY ACTIVITY IDEAS

THIS WEEK'S CHALLENGES

THIS WEEK'S HIGHLIGHTS

OTHER COMMENTS

WEEK 45:
GOALS & OVERVIEW

SPEECH & COMMUNICATION

SOCIAL SKILLS

SENSORY & O.T.

APPOINTMENTS

MONDAY:

TUESDAY:

WEDNESDAY:

THURSDAY:

FRIDAY:

SATURDAY:

SUNDAY:

FINE MOTOR:

VESTIBULAR/PROPRIOCEPTIVE:

TACTILE:

VISUAL:

ORAL MOTOR:

AUDITORY:

SPEECH & LANGUAGE:

SOCIAL SKILLS:

SENSORY & THERAPY ACTIVITY IDEAS

WEEK 45:
IDEAS & REVIEW

THIS WEEK'S CHALLENGES

THIS WEEK'S HIGHLIGHTS

OTHER COMMENTS

WEEK 46:
GOALS & OVERVIEW

SPEECH & COMMUNICATION

SOCIAL SKILLS

SENSORY & O.T.

APPOINTMENTS

MONDAY:

TUESDAY:

WEDNESDAY:

THURSDAY:

FRIDAY:

SATURDAY:

SUNDAY:

WEEK 46:
IDEAS & REVIEW

FINE MOTOR:

VESTIBULAR/PROPRIOCEPTIVE:

TACTILE:

VISUAL:

ORAL MOTOR:

AUDITORY:

SPEECH & LANGUAGE:

SOCIAL SKILLS:

SENSORY & THERAPY ACTIVITY IDEAS

THIS WEEK'S CHALLENGES

THIS WEEK'S HIGHLIGHTS

OTHER COMMENTS

WEEK 47:
GOALS & OVERVIEW

SPEECH & COMMUNICATION

SOCIAL SKILLS

SENSORY & O.T.

APPOINTMENTS

MONDAY:

TUESDAY:

WEDNESDAY:

THURSDAY:

FRIDAY:

SATURDAY:

SUNDAY:

FINE MOTOR:

VESTIBULAR/PROPRIOCEPTIVE:

TACTILE:

VISUAL:

ORAL MOTOR:

AUDITORY:

SPEECH & LANGUAGE:

SOCIAL SKILLS:

SENSORY & THERAPY ACTIVITY IDEAS

WEEK 47:
IDEAS & REVIEW

THIS WEEK'S CHALLENGES

THIS WEEK'S HIGHLIGHTS

OTHER COMMENTS

WEEK 48:
GOALS & OVERVIEW

SPEECH & COMMUNICATION

SOCIAL SKILLS

SENSORY & O.T.

APPOINTMENTS

MONDAY:

TUESDAY:

WEDNESDAY:

THURSDAY:

FRIDAY:

SATURDAY:

SUNDAY:

FINE MOTOR:

VESTIBULAR/PROPRIOCEPTIVE:

TACTILE:

VISUAL:

ORAL MOTOR:

AUDITORY:

SPEECH & LANGUAGE:

SOCIAL SKILLS:

SENSORY & THERAPY ACTIVITY IDEAS

THIS WEEK'S CHALLENGES

THIS WEEK'S HIGHLIGHTS

OTHER COMMENTS

WEEK 49:
GOALS & OVERVIEW

SPEECH & COMMUNICATION

SOCIAL SKILLS

SENSORY & O.T.

APPOINTMENTS

MONDAY:

TUESDAY:

WEDNESDAY:

THURSDAY:

FRIDAY:

SATURDAY:

SUNDAY:

FINE MOTOR:

VESTIBULAR/PROPRIOCEPTIVE:

TACTILE:

VISUAL:

ORAL MOTOR:

AUDITORY:

SPEECH & LANGUAGE:

SOCIAL SKILLS:

SENSORY & THERAPY ACTIVITY IDEAS

THIS WEEK'S CHALLENGES

THIS WEEK'S HIGHLIGHTS

OTHER COMMENTS

WEEK 50:
GOALS & OVERVIEW

SPEECH & COMMUNICATION

SOCIAL SKILLS

SENSORY & O.T.

APPOINTMENTS

MONDAY:

TUESDAY:

WEDNESDAY:

THURSDAY:

FRIDAY:

SATURDAY:

SUNDAY:

WEEK 50:
IDEAS & REVIEW

FINE MOTOR:

VESTIBULAR/PROPRIOCEPTIVE:

TACTILE:

VISUAL:

ORAL MOTOR:

AUDITORY:

SPEECH & LANGUAGE:

SOCIAL SKILLS:

SENSORY & THERAPY ACTIVITY IDEAS

THIS WEEK'S CHALLENGES

THIS WEEK'S HIGHLIGHTS

OTHER COMMENTS

WEEK 51:
GOALS & OVERVIEW

SPEECH & COMMUNICATION

SOCIAL SKILLS

SENSORY & O.T.

APPOINTMENTS

MONDAY:

TUESDAY:

WEDNESDAY:

THURSDAY:

FRIDAY:

SATURDAY:

SUNDAY:

FINE MOTOR:

VESTIBULAR/PROPRIOCEPTIVE:

TACTILE:

VISUAL:

ORAL MOTOR:

AUDITORY:

SPEECH & LANGUAGE:

SOCIAL SKILLS:

SENSORY & THERAPY ACTIVITY IDEAS

THIS WEEK'S CHALLENGES

THIS WEEK'S HIGHLIGHTS

OTHER COMMENTS

WEEK 52:
GOALS & OVERVIEW

SPEECH & COMMUNICATION

SOCIAL SKILLS

SENSORY & O.T.

APPOINTMENTS

MONDAY:

TUESDAY:

WEDNESDAY:

THURSDAY:

FRIDAY:

SATURDAY:

SUNDAY:

FINE MOTOR:

VESTIBULAR/PROPRIOCEPTIVE:

TACTILE:

VISUAL:

ORAL MOTOR:

AUDITORY:

SPEECH & LANGUAGE:

SOCIAL SKILLS:

SENSORY & THERAPY ACTIVITY IDEAS

WEEK 52:
IDEAS & REVIEW

THIS WEEK'S CHALLENGES

THIS WEEK'S HIGHLIGHTS

OTHER COMMENTS

MORE AUTISM RESOURCES:
GET HELP FILLING OUT THIS WORKBOOK

If you need help filling in your autism planner workbook, please visit And Next Comes L at **http://www.andnextcomesL.com** where you can subscribe to the free weekly autism planner newsletter. Each week you will receive an email with a list of activity ideas, practical tips, printables, app suggestions, and more that will help you plan out your child's week with ease.

Made in United States
North Haven, CT
15 April 2022

18310653R00063